THE
10
TM

Most Amazing Adaptations in Nature

Christopher J. Reaume • Laura E. Harrison

Series Editor
Jeffrey D. Wilhelm

Much thought, debate, and research went into choosing and ranking the 10 items in each book in this series. We realize that everyone has his or her own opinion of what is most significant, revolutionary, amazing, deadly, and so on. As you read, you may agree with our choices, or you may be surprised — and that's the way it should be!

an imprint of

SCHOLASTIC

www.scholastic.com/librarypublishing

A Rubicon book published in association with Scholastic Inc.

Ru'bĭcon © 2007 Rubicon Publishing Inc.
www.rubiconpublishing.com

 is a trademark of The 10 Books

Associate Publishers: Kim Koh, Miriam Bardswich
Project Editor: Amy Land
Editor: Elizabeth Siegel
Creative Director: Jennifer Drew
Project Manager/Designer: Jeanette MacLean
Graphic Designer: Brandon Köpke

The publisher gratefully acknowledges the following for permission to reprint copyrighted material in this book.

Every reasonable effort has been made to trace the owners of copyrighted material and to make due acknowledgment. Any errors or omissions drawn to our attention will be gladly rectified in future editions.

"Pangolin strays into village!" From *The Hindu*, September 5, 2005. Permission courtesy of N. Ram, Editor-in-Chief, *The Hindu*. Used with permission.

Cover image: Penguins–Getty Images/Digital Vision/David Tipling

Library and Archives Canada Cataloguing in Publication

The 10 most amazing adaptations in nature/Christopher J. Reaume and Laura E. Harrison.

Includes index.
ISBN 978-1-55448-461-4

    1. Readers (Elementary) 2. Readers—Nature. I. Harrison, Laura E
II. Title. III. Title: Ten most amazing adaptations in nature.

PE1117.R437 2007   428.6   C2007-900553-5

1 2 3 4 5 6 7 8 9 10   10   16 15 14 13 12 11 10 09 08 07

Printed in Singapore

Contents

6

26

34

SURVIVAL OF THE FITTEST!

You do it all the time. You adapt when you move to a new neighborhood, go to a new school, or make a new friend. You adjust to make things work.

Like you, animals and plants adapt, too, but for different reasons. They do it to find food and shelter, to reproduce, and even to protect themselves. Some adaptations are behavioral, like penguins using instincts to make their nests. Others are genetic, like bats using sound to move around and find prey. The animals and plants on our list of adaptations have all developed cool tools or slick tricks to survive in their environment. It is one sure way not to become extinct like the dinosaurs.

Think like a naturalist, and look around you. What are some specific adaptations of animals and plants that help them to succeed in their environment? Animals adapt mainly through genetic changes that alter their behavior, coloring, or physical appearance. Which of these is a more amazing adaptation: a fish with its own built-in fishing rod or an animal that shows up complete with its own armor and stink bombs?

In this book, we present what we think are the 10 most amazing adaptations in nature. The features we describe evolved after millions of years. Some adaptations help animals or plants protect themselves from prey; some help them survive in harsh environments. Others include unique mating habits. As you read through our list, ask yourself:

naturalist: *scientist who studies nature*

WHICH IS
THE MOST AMAZING
ADAPTATION
OF ALL?

10 HAWK MOTHS

The hawk moth's wings beat so fast that they make a humming sound (just like a hummingbird).

HAWK MOTH–SHUTTERSTOCK

6

DESCRIPTION: Insect, any group of sleek-looking moths named for their swift flight patterns

COOL TOOL: Super-long tongues that can reach the sugary nectar at the bottom of deep tubular flowers

Imagine if your tongue reached down to your feet. Well, a hawk moth's tongue (called a proboscis) is often many times longer than its body! Take the giant hawk moth, for instance. Its proboscis is over seven inches long. Luckily, these moths can curl their tongues into a spiral so they don't get "tongue-tied."

The amazing tongue of the hawk moth allows it to reach down to the bottom of deep tubular flowers (like lilies and orchids) to get nectar that other insects can't reach. It's no coincidence that hawk moths seem to be made for these flowers. Both changed together over time in a process called coevolution. As the tubes of flowers got deeper, the tongues of the moths grew longer.

This happened because hawk moths and tubular flowers depend on each other for survival. Flowers are usually both male and female and are brightly colored to attract insects to help them carry pollen from flower to flower. The flowers provide hawk moths with pollen, which is their food. The hawk moths move pollen from the male flowers to the female flowers so they can reproduce. Not a bad trade-off!

 Hawk moths and tubular flowers depend on each other to survive. Name other plants and animals in nature that have similar relationships.

HAWK MOTHS

LOOKING GOOD!

Hawk moths start off as eggs and develop into caterpillars (commonly known as hornworms). Adult moths have streamlined bodies and narrow wings. Depending on the type, hawk moths vary in color and have wingspans of one to six inches.

---

streamlined: *smoothly shaped; narrow*

Quick Fact

Before hawk moths were discovered, the great naturalist Charles Darwin predicted that there must be animals with super-long tongues. He figured some kind of animal must have developed a way to reach the nectar found in deep tubular flowers. People made fun of his idea, but 21 years later he was proven right when the hawk moth was discovered.

Quick Fact

Hawk moths are some of the world's fastest flying insects. They can fly over 30 mph. That's faster than a jackrabbit can run.

WHERE IN THE WORLD?

Hawk moths can be found in almost all parts of the world, but most of the 1,200 different kinds are found in the tropics. Hawk moths are nocturnal, so look for them at night.

FINE DINING

Pass the poison please! In the caterpillar stage, many kinds of hawk moths like to dine on toxic tree leaves. But the poison doesn't seem to hurt these hardy insects. It simply oozes out of their bodies before it can affect them. Adult hawk moths eat only nectar from flowers.

SURVIVAL KIT

In addition to its super-long, nectar-slurping tongue, a hawk moth is a fabulous flier. Some hawk moths can hover in midair while feeding from flowers, in the same way that a hummingbird can. They can also move quickly from side to side to avoid predators.

? Sometimes a hawk moth is mistaken for a hummingbird, despite one being an insect and the other a bird. Why do you think this is?

The Expert Says...

" To protect itself, the hawk moth has two very simple ears on its mouth that are exposed when it extends its proboscis to feed. If the moth hears a bat, it immediately flies away before the bat knows that it's there. Many other night-flying insects also have ears to listen for the cries of hunting bats, but none are as simple as those of the hawk moth. "

— Dr. James Fullard, professor, University of Toronto

10 9 8 7 6

MADE FOR EACH OTHER

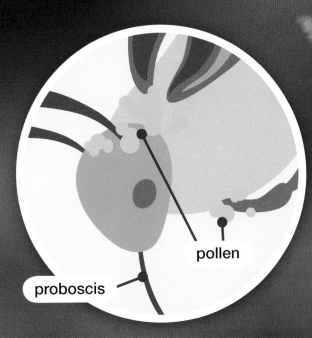

proboscis

pollen

This diagram shows how plants have developed so that their pollen doesn't get wasted on the wrong species. When a hawk moth goes to get nectar from a flower, the plant's pollen rubs off on a very specific part of the moth (orange in the diagram above). That means if the moth goes to a flower of the same species, the pollen is in the right place to rub off on the flower's pistil. But if the moth goes to a different kind of flower, the pollen isn't in the right place to connect with the pistil. It will stay on the moth until it visits the right kind of flower.

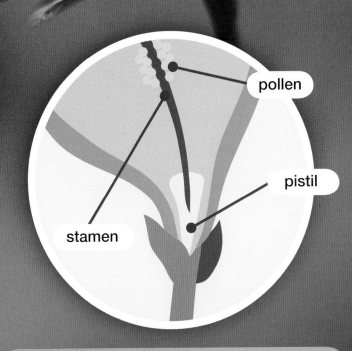

pollen

pistil

stamen

 Hawk moths have evolved a special body part to help them get their food. What other insects or animals have a specialized body part to help them get their grub?

Quick Fact

On your marks, get set, shiver! Most hawk moths shiver to warm up their muscles before going into flight. Once in the air, they really get a workout and their body temperatures can almost double to reach 105°F.

Take Note

For an animal to survive, it needs to be able to get food. The hawk moth is #10 because it developed a long tongue to collect nectar from flowers that other insects couldn't reach. How's that for licking a problem?
- The hawk moth isn't the only insect that has come up with amazing ways to feed. Give another example. Do you think your example deserves to replace the hawk moth at #10 on our list? Explain your answer.

5   4   3   2   1

9 CARNIVOROUS

The Venus flytrap in midsnack — YUM!

PLANTS

DESCRIPTION: Sometimes called insectivorous plants, they get their nutrients from trapping and eating insects and other small animals

COOL TOOL: Bug-catching traps — in all shapes and sizes

You probably already know about the Venus flytrap. But did you know that there are other bug-catching plants out there, too? Some have tentacles. Some make their own "glue." Others, like the bladderwort, use a built-in vacuum to suck in their prey. They might sound like something out of a science-fiction movie, but these plants are the real deal.

Carnivorous plants are tough. Many of them grow in poor soils that don't have enough food to support regular plants. So these plants have found their own unique ways to get extra nutrients. Their adaptations allow them to catch and eat insects. If the plants are big enough, they can even eat frogs!

carnivorous: *meat-eating*

CARNIVOROUS PLANTS

LOOKING GOOD!

Carnivorous plants come in many shapes and sizes. Some look like regular garden plants. Others are quite bizarre and look like water pitchers or have gaping jaws ready to snap shut like a clam.

WHERE IN THE WORLD?

There are about 600 different kinds of carnivorous plants found around the world. That's not many considering there are hundreds of thousands of different plants out there. Bug-catching plants tend to be found in places like bogs — where there's a lot of sun and water, but poor soil.

Bladderworts

FINE DINING

Meat-eating plants usually eat insects. However, some carnivorous plants also eat spiders and small reptiles such as frogs and lizards.

SURVIVAL KIT

Different carnivorous plants have come up with different ways of catching bugs. Scientists have given names to these types of traps: pitfall traps, flypaper traps, snap traps, bladder traps, and lobster-pot traps. As you can tell from their names, humans use similar kinds of traps to catch things, too!

? Why do you think there are so few carnivorous plants in the plant world?

Quick Fact

Follow your nose. At least that's what some kinds of pitcher plants count on insects to do. The plants produce a sweet nectar to attract insects. When the insect lands, it falls into the pitcher part of the plant where it's digested.

Quick Fact

A bladderwort has a small water-filled sac, or bladder, that acts like a vacuum when the water is pumped out of it. First, an insect steps on little hairs growing over a "trapdoor" on the plant. Then the trap door opens and whoosh! The bladder sucks the insect inside the plant to be digested.

The Expert Says...

" I explore bogs and swamps around the world to study carnivorous plants. Once, while photographing bladderworts, I discovered that two separate plants had sucked the opposite ends of a long worm into their traps. It was like two diners fighting over a single strand of spaghetti! Over seven days, they slowly gobbled up the worm from opposite ends. "

— Dr. Barry A. Rice, invasive species specialist, The Nature Conservancy

A bumblebee investigates a pitcher plant — a little too close for comfort!

ALL IMAGES SHUTTERSTOCK

Snap!

This report describes how these tricky plants work.

Flies can move fast when they want to. Spiders can move even faster. But that's nothing compared to the speed of snap-trap plants that can catch them. Only two kinds of carnivorous plants use a snap trap — the Venus flytrap and the waterwheel plant — and they're both good at catching their prey.

The leaves on these plants have developed into two connected round bits (called lobes) that look a little like an open clam. Inside these lobes are little hairs, called trigger hairs, that react when touched. If a small insect bends these hairs, a signal is sent from the hair to the part of the leaf where the two lobes join. This causes the lobes to snap together in a split second like a clam shutting its shell.

Snap-trap plants actually have a simple form of memory. Just tapping once won't close their lobes. Otherwise, they would be opening and closing again every time it rained. Instead, it takes two touches to the lobes within 30 seconds before the trap closes. Pretty smart for a plant!

Once the prey is trapped, the closed lobes do an amazing thing. They turn into a stomach! They start to ooze digestive juices, like the ones found in a human stomach. This slowly dissolves the prey's soft inner parts over the next week or so. If the prey is an insect with a hard shell, the crunchy bits get washed away by the next rain after the leaves reopen. Then the plant is ready to grab its next bite!

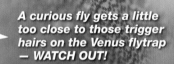

A curious fly gets a little too close to those trigger hairs on the Venus flytrap — WATCH OUT!

Take Note

By adding insects to their diets, carnivorous plants are able to survive in poor soil conditions where many other plants can't. We were impressed enough with these plants' "can-do" attitude and clever bug-catching traps to put them at #9 on our list.

- Despite carnivorous plants' great bug-catching traps, they still have to wait for their food to come to them. Do you think their lack of mobility makes them less amazing than the hawk moth? Or do you agree that these determined plants deserve to be at #9 on our list? Why or why not?

8 PANGOLINS

The pangolin has an extra long tongue that's perfect for slurping up ants and termites.

DESCRIPTION: Mammal of the Pholidota family; also known as scaly anteaters

COOL TOOL: A super-long, sticky, mucus-covered tongue for gobbling up bugs

Pangolins (Pan-go-lins) have been described as a cross between a lizard and a giant pinecone. They're also kind of cute. But don't let their innocent appearance fool you. They have a serious set of survival equipment that is perfect for a place teeming with insects.

For starters, a pangolin has huge front claws for destroying insect nests. Its extra long tongue is perfect for slurping up ants and termites from these nests. Throw in its tough scales that keep the bugs from biting and you've got the ultimate insect eater! And did we mention that a pangolin can spray stinky liquid as a skunk does. It also can roll up in a ball when it senses danger. This covers its vulnerable parts, like its face and belly, with its scaly tail. The edges of the pangolin's scales are razor sharp to keep its enemies from trying to unroll it. Not bad for a walking pinecone!

The pangolin's body design is perfect for eating termites and ants, but insect cocoons may be a bit trickier. If you were to design a mammal that ate butterfly and moth cocoons, what would it look like and why?

PANGOLINS

LOOKING GOOD!

A pangolin has a small head, a long tongue, a long tail, and a lot of scales. In fact, its scales make up about one-fifth of its total weight, which is usually 30 to 40 pounds for common pangolins. Pangolins walk on their short hind legs with their backs hunched over because the claws on their forelimbs are difficult to walk on.

Quick Fact

The common pangolin's wormlike tongue can extend to about 10 inches. But that's nothing compared to its relative, the giant pangolin. The pangolin's tongue is about two feet long!

WHERE IN THE WORLD?

Eight species of pangolins live in parts of Africa and Southeast Asia. Pangolins live in forests and grasslands where there are a lot of bugs.

FINE DINING

Pangolins go buggy for bugs — especially ants and termites. They have an amazing sense of smell to help them sniff out dinner. Pangolins are nocturnal animals that look for their food after dark. One pangolin can eat as many as 200,000 ants in a night!

? Pangolins have an amazing sense of smell and hearing. Why might this be more important to a pangolin than having good vision?

SURVIVAL KIT

As we said, a pangolin is well equipped with its sharp front claws, armor-like scales, stinky spray, and long tongue. Its tongue is sticky, too — thanks to extra-big salivary glands that coat its tongue with a gummy, mucus-type of spit!

mucus: *thick, slippery substance*

Quick Fact

Pangolins do a good job of protecting themselves in the wild, but are still easy prey for humans. Some societies hunt pangolins for their meat or to use their scales in medicines or potions. This hunting, along with the destruction of their habitat, has endangered some kinds of pangolins.

The Expert Says...

" If the attacker attempts to unroll it, the pangolin lashes out with the tail, using it as a club and attempting to inflict cuts on its attacker with the razor-sharp scales. "

— Heike Schütze, author of *Field Guide to the Mammals of the Kruger National Park*

A pangolin enjoying some ants from a rotten tree stump

8

7   6

Pangolin strays into village!

Article from *The Hindu*, Staff Correspondent, September 5, 2005

BIDAR, INDIA: A pangolin strayed into a farmer's house … on Saturday night. People were confused as many had not seen such an animal before.

A few villagers who saw its snakelike tongue thought it was poisonous. Some others thought it belonged to the family of porcupines.

The animal curled up under a car and stayed there for hours. Villagers told presspersons that they were unable to get the animal to come out from under the car. "The stick bounced back when it hit the animal's body. The scales on its body are as strong as concrete," said Mardan Mian, in whose house the pangolin was found.

A team of forest officials arrived at the village and captured the animal. They later released it in the forests in Honnaddi.

Deputy Conservator of Forests P.C. Ray said it is common for wild animals to enter villages

A few villagers who saw its snakelike tongue thought it was poisonous.

looking for food. Pangolins eat ants and cannot be reared in captivity.

They do not survive even in zoos, he said. Mr. Ray said that pangolins are harmless and nonpoisonous. He appealed to the people not to panic if they see a wild animal. He urged them not to attack or kill any wild animal, and inform the forest office if they come across animals in villages. …

Quick Fact

The name "pangolin" comes from a Malaysian word that means "something that rolls up." Makes sense!

Take Note

Anteaters and aardvarks may have a few features similar to a pangolin's. However, none has the complete set of survival equipment that a pangolin, our #8 choice, has. After all, would you mess with an animal that sprays like a skunk and has razor-sharp scales?

• Do you think the number of adaptations each animal has makes it more amazing? Or do you think how the adaptations work is more important? Explain.

5   2   1

A gray whale scoop feeds on the ocean bottom.

GRAY WHALE—© BOB CRANSTON/ANIMALS ANIMALS

LES

DESCRIPTION: A type of mammal of the suborder Cetacea (whales, dolphins, porpoises), also known as the great whale

COOL TOOL: Plates for eating with ... but not the kind you put on the dinner table. A baleen whale's feeding plates strain the water out of its food.

What do a hippo and a whale have in common? That might sound like a riddle, but the real answer is that they are relatives. Really! Experts believe that whales, like hippos, evolved from hoofed animals that lived on Earth millions of years ago. That's one amazing makeover!

Once in the water, these animals evolved into enormous creatures. Although there are no "shrimps" in the whale family, the largest kind are baleen whales. In fact, one of these, the blue whale, is the largest animal to ever live on Earth. (Yep, it's even bigger than dinosaurs were!) Their massive size means that, other than humans, they have few enemies.

Baleen whales get their name from the baleen plates they have in their mouths. They use these plates instead of teeth for feeding. These big beasts don't need huge choppers because they like to eat tiny sea creatures. The baleen acts like a strainer. It keeps the small yummy stuff in their mouths and strains out the water and everything else. It's a handy tool for picky eaters!

 If this mammal did not have baleen plates, what problem might it face?

BALEEN WHALES

LOOKING GOOD!

Baleen whales are characterized by having baleen plates for filtering food from water, rather than having teeth. These guys are big! They are torpedo-shaped and tend to be black or gray. (In case you were wondering, blue whales are actually blue-gray!)

WHERE IN THE WORLD?

A few of the 14 or so types of baleen whales don't wander much. But the rest of them can be found all over the world's oceans. In fact, some gray whales make 12,000-mile round-trips to feeding and mating areas across the globe!

? Why do you think the world's biggest animal lives in the sea instead of on land?

FINE DINING

These massive mammals eat some of the tiniest creatures around, like krill and plankton ... but they need a lot of them! The blue whale can eat up to 8,000 pounds of krill in one day. Most baleen whales spend the summer feeding heavily and then live off their blubber (fat supplies) during the winter months.

krill: *tiny shrimplike creatures*
plankton: *very tiny animal and plant life*

? Many whales eat very specific foods. The giant blue whale, for instance, survives almost only on krill. How does being a picky eater put an animal at a higher risk of extinction?

Quick Fact

All baleen whales make sounds, but two of them — the humpback whale and the blue whale — are known for singing elaborate "songs." Scientists think this may serve to strengthen friendships among groups of whales and to help attract mates.

SURVIVAL KIT

In addition to its super size and cool feeding manner, a baleen whale is an awesome diver. It can stay underwater without taking a breath for up to 35 minutes. It can do this because its blood carries high levels of oxygen to its lungs, heart, and brain while it is underwater.

Quick Fact

Fossils show us that the ancestors of baleen whales had teeth. About 25 to 30 million years ago, their hairy fringes of baleen began to appear and their teeth started to disappear. Today, baby baleen whales still go through a stage while they are inside their mothers' wombs where they have tiny teeth. These teeth disappear before they are born.

The gentle giant — a humpback whale glides gracefully through water.

The Expert Says...

" In one sense, evolution didn't invent anything new with whales. It was just tinkering with land mammals. It's using the old to make the new. "

— Dr. Neil Shubin, evolutionary biologist and professor, University of Chicago

tinkering: *experimenting*

A WHALE OF AN APPETITE

THIS REPORT EXPLAINS HOW THESE GIANTS EAT.

Baleen whales include the gray whale, the bowhead whale, and the humpback whale. What do they have in common? They all love to eat krill. But here's the problem: a krill weighs about as much as a thumbtack. A blue whale weighs about as much as 10 elephants. So baleen whales need to literally eat tons of krill and plankton to fill their huge bellies. To feed this appetite, baleen whales are constantly looking for food during their feeding season (in the summer months). That's where their baleen plates come in. These plates are attached to a baleen whale's upper jaw and look a bit like combs with hairy tips. (Baleen plates are made of the same material as your nails and hair, so they are both stiff and elastic.) Here's how they work:

A gray whale skim-feeding

- The whale swims along the water's surface, taking in large amounts of fish, water, and debris, which may include plants, leaves, or shells.

- A baleen whale has grooves in its throat that expand when it takes in a big mouthful of food and water. These then contract and the whale pushes the water and debris out of its mouth with its immense tongue.

This baleen plate is made up of tiny hairs that trap fish and plankton.

- The water is forced out through the baleen plates. These plates act like a filter. They keep the krill and plankton in and let the water out. When the water is gone, the whale swallows the food left in its mouth and starts looking for its next "bite"!

Take Note

It's pretty amazing that the largest living animals feed on the smallest ones in the sea. Baleen whales can do this thanks to their baleen feeding plates. These whales hold the #7 spot on our list.
- Imagine you've been transformed into a sea animal, but you still look like yourself. What three things would you change about your body to help you survive in your new environment? Give your reasons.

6 PENGUINS

Emperor penguins waddling out of the icy water

DESCRIPTION: A type of aquatic, flightless bird found in the Southern Hemisphere

COOL TOOL: They have wings that are built for swimming instead of flying. The penguin spends more time in the water than any other bird!

Penguins. Sure, they're kind of cute. They've been in movies like *Happy Feet* and *March of the Penguins* and can be found in most zoos. But is there anything amazing about them? The answer is "yes!" After all, what other bird can swim but can't fly? And how many other animals can survive the cold of Antarctica?

Penguins spend over half their time in the water. Their wings make perfect paddles to help them steer and they can go fast. Their top swimming speed can hit 15 mph. That's about as fast as you can run!

Most penguins can handle the cold, too. Take the emperor penguin. These hardy animals live through winter in the Antarctic where the temperature can get down to -22°F. *Brrr!* To survive, emperor penguins have come up with some unique behaviors. They stay warm by huddling together in large groups and even take turns being on the outside of the huddle where it is the coldest. They also keep their eggs off the cold ice by balancing them on their feet. (Guess that keeps them on their toes!)

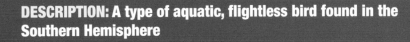

Penguins are the most social bird species. They gather together on land in groups, as well as swim and feed in groups in the water. Why do you think this is?

PENGUINS

LOOKING GOOD!

Penguins look like overstuffed birds with small heads and short wings. They have a dark (usually black) head and back, and a white underside. This is to help them hide from predators. When sea lions or killer whales are swimming underneath the penguin, its white belly blends in with the light surface of the water. From above, a penguin's dark back blends in with the dark water below.

Quick Fact

Penguins come in many sizes. The smallest kind, the fairy penguin, would barely reach your knees. The largest kind, the emperor penguin, grows to about 45 inches and can weigh up to 100 pounds!

WHERE IN THE WORLD?

Most kinds of penguins live in the cold waters of the world's southern oceans. But, there are a couple of species that can be found as far north as the equator.

There are 17 species of penguins living from the Antarctic to the equator. What kinds of physical differences do you think you'd see between the penguins that live in the Antarctic and those in a warmer climate?

FINE DINING

Penguins go where the food is — in the water! They eat fish, krill, and squid.

A Magellanic penguin catching dinner!

SURVIVAL KIT

On land, a penguin can look awkward getting around. But the penguin is in its element in the water. Its "wings" act like flippers and its watertight feathers hold in a layer of warm air to help the penguin float and keep it warm.

Quick Fact

Penguins migrate like other birds, but they swim or march instead of fly. In fact, Magellanic penguins can swim over 90 miles in a day, dive to 300 feet, and migrate more than 2,000 nautical miles [2,300 miles] from their breeding grounds to their wintering grounds!

A colony of gentoo penguins guarding nests in the Antarctic

Quick Fact

Most penguins live in places where plants are scarce. So instead of using twigs to build a nest, they use pebbles and penguin poop!

Birds of a Feather

This comparison chart points out the differences between penguins and most other birds.

Specialized glands to get rid of excess salt taken in from seawater

Sharp vision to spot food from high in air

Large feathers on wings for flying

Eyes to see underwater

Very little body fat

Torpedo-shaped body to move easily through the water

Watertight feathers are small and overlap one another; dark back/white belly acts as camouflage in the water

Large chest with strong flight muscles concentrated in one area

Except for waterfowl, most birds have claw-like feet.

Flippers for swimming

Blubber (fat) to keep out the cold

Light skeleton (hollow bones) to allow it to fly

Heavy skeleton (solid bones) to allow it to stay underwater

Webbed feet for steering in the water

The Expert Says...

"Magellanic penguins' eggshells are the thickest of the seabirds and females ingest old shells before egg-laying presumably because they need calcium. They also ingest rocks to help them grind up their food because they don't have gizzards."

— Dr. Dee Boersma, University of Washington

gizzards: *sacs behind the stomach where food is broken down into small particles*

Take Note

We just had to find a spot on our list for a bird that prefers the water to the air! Think of all the adaptations the penguin's ancestors had to do. They went from living on land to being able to soar through the air. Then they evolved some more to handle the water. (The great whale at #7 evolved from land to water without the extra step that penguins took.) That and the cool ways some penguins developed to survive the cold put them at #6.

• The penguin species hasn't changed much in 45 million years. Why do you think this is? What does this say about its adaptations?

5   4   3   2   1

5 ANGLERFISH

The netdevil anglerfish has a glowing structure shaped like an upside-down tree under its chin.

A fish that fishes? That's right. This fish brings its own fishing equipment wherever it goes. An "angler" is someone who fishes with a hook and line, which means the anglerfish is well named. You won't believe how it fishes for its dinner.

Most anglerfish live deep in the ocean. It's so dark down there that it's impossible to see the tip of your own nose — never mind trying to find food! But these fish have a glowing "lantern" hanging right over their mouths that also acts like bait on a fishing rod. Hungry fish are attracted to the glow, swim up to check things out, and — *gulp!* — they become the anglerfish's dinner.

That's not the only amazing feature on an anglerfish. They have one of the strangest ways of mating ever. (Hint: It's not great to be a male anglerfish!) Read on to learn more about this fascinating fish …

ANGLERFISH

LOOKING GOOD!

An anglerfish looks like a balloon with a monster mouth full of teeth. These fish range from quite small to several feet long. The female anglerfish is always larger than the male. The female anglerfish also has a long growth near its mouth that it can wiggle to attract other fish. Depending on the species, this "lure" can vary in size and grow from different parts of the female's body. In deep-sea anglerfish, the lure is usually bioluminescent.

bioluminescent: *living thing that glows*

WHERE IN THE WORLD?

Anglerfish can be found in oceans all over the world. Most kinds live in extremely deep water — from 1,500 to 7,000 feet. That's deeper than most submarines can go.

FINE DINING

Adult anglerfish eat any type of fish that is unlucky enough to go near them. The size of the fish usually isn't a problem. An anglerfish has a stretchable stomach, jaws, and ribs, so it can swallow prey twice its own size!

SURVIVAL KIT

The anglerfish's best tool has to be its glowing lure. It attracts other fish so it can then gobble them up. This lure also helps to attract a potential mate. But the anglerfish doesn't make the lure glow by itself. The lure is actually home to millions of bacteria that produce light with the chemicals they make.

The fan fin anglerfish is found in subtropical and tropical waters at depths of 650 to 1,300 feet.

The bacteria that make the anglerfish's lure glow are bioluminescent. Can you think of any other bioluminescent animals? What type of environment would you expect them to live in?

Anglerfish are often gray, brown, or black so they can't be seen in the glow of their own light. Why do you think not being seen is important?

The Expert Says...

As part of my research work I tagged and released anglerfish around the Shetland Islands [at the north end of the UK]. One fish was recaptured off Iceland [545 miles], one off Faroe [200 miles], and one off Norway [185 miles]. Nobody knew that these fish could swim so far!

— Dr. Chevonne Laurenson, lecturer and researcher, North Atlantic Fisheries College, UK

LOVE AT FIRST BITE

ANGLERFISH PHOTOS—©PETER DAVID/GETTY IMAGES; CHEVONNE LAURENSON—COURTESY CHEVONNE LAURENSON; ALL OTHER IMAGES—SHUTTERSTOCK, ISTOCKPHOTO

Quick Fact

The male of one kind of anglerfish, the *Photocorynus spiniceps*, is the smallest known animal with a backbone. It's only about 0.2 inches long. The female of this species is no shrimp. It's about 10 times bigger than the male!

The male anglerfish can be seen here as it is absorbed into the female!

Some animals need to find a new mate every season. Other kinds, like many ducks or the albatross, find a partner and mate for life. This step-by-step report explains how the anglerfish "mates for life."

CHECK THIS OUT!

○ Finding a mate in the vast, dark, deep sea isn't easy. So the male anglerfish uses his well-developed sense of smell to find a female. The female helps him out by releasing a kind of perfume into the water. Her glowing lure also makes her easier to spot.

○ Once a male anglerfish finds a female, he grips her skin with his strong teeth and locks on.

○ What happens next is really strange! The male begins to disintegrate! His jaws become glued to the female's skin. Then his eyes start to shrink until they're gone. His blood vessels link to those of the female so he can nourish himself through her. That's actually a good thing for the male because male anglerfish don't have a digestive system and can't eat by themselves.

○ After this, the rest of the male's insides disappear. All that remains are his organs that release sperm when the female is ready to release an egg. In an amazing feat of nature, the male and female have become one. Now the anglerfish can produce eggs that will be instantly fertilized. Her dating problems are solved!

Take Note

We ranked this freaky fish #5 on our list because its adaptations allow it to live successfully in a place where most other animals cannot survive.
• The anglerfish is a bony fish that has adapted to its unique environment. If you could live in an extreme environment, where would you choose? Think of a feature that would help you adapt to this climate.

5   **4**   **3**   **2**   **1**

The front feet of the Surinam toad are not webbed. They have fingers instead.

DESCRIPTION: A type of amphibian from a family of primitive, tongueless frogs native to South America

COOL TOOL: The mother Surinam toad has a handy-dandy built-in egg carton. She carries her eggs around on her back!

This frog is freaky! Yep, the Surinam (Suh-rah-naam) toad is actually a frog because toads live mostly on land. This critter doesn't follow the crowd. Unlike other frogs, it doesn't have a tongue and bulgy eyes. It doesn't go *rrr-i-bbitt* and its front feet have long, alien-like fingers that aren't webbed like other frogs.

It doesn't even come out of the water. Most other frogs are amphibious. But the Surinam toad is completely aquatic (it lives its entire life in the water).

This frog starts its life off in a unique way too. A mother Surinam toad doesn't just deposit her eggs somewhere and split. Instead, she carries her eggs around on her back until they are ready to hatch and hop away. These funny frogs completely skip being tadpoles. And wait until you hear about how the mom gets the eggs on her back in the first place …

amphibious: *living on both land and in the water; most frogs are amphibians*

Why do you think the Surinam toad has so many features that are different from other kinds of frogs?

SURINAM TOAD–©E. R. DEGGINGER/ANIMALS ANIMALS

SURINAM TOADS

LOOKING GOOD!

This frog looks like a rectangular pancake with legs. Its back is green-brown and its belly is white. You can tell when you come across a mother Surinam toad because the eggs she is carrying around on her back look like great big zits!

WHERE IN THE WORLD?

Surinam toads come from Surinam, a country in South America. They often live in water that is muddy or even polluted. The murky water helps them hide out from predators.

FINE DINING

This frog is not a picky eater. It eats fish, worms, and small shellfish. It can't see too well in the muddy water, so it swims with its arms in front of it, gobbling up whatever animals it touches.

? Why do you think it doesn't matter too much that the Surinam toad doesn't have good vision? How do humans with limited vision adapt?

SURVIVAL KIT

Besides its cool way of carrying its eggs around, a Surinam toad has good camouflage. Its flat body and the green-brown color on its back blend in well with a muddy lake bottom. To prey beneath it, the frog's white belly looks the same color as the water's surface. Plus, this toad's front feet have actual fingers with sensitive star-shaped organs that help them find and catch prey.

The Surinam toad is an aquatic animal, but it doesn't have gills. It needs to go up to the surface once in a while to get air.

10

9

6

AN EGG-CITING STORY

So how does the mother Surinam toad get her eggs on her back? This report explains ...

- When it's time to breed, the male Surinam toad makes clicking sounds in the water to attract a female.

- After they've made contact, the male grabs the female around her waist and holds her tightly. This can last for several hours!

- Then come the gymnastics. The male and female perform a sort of a dance with somersaults and flips. During this dance, the female drops her eggs and the male fertilizes them. As with most fish and amphibians, this occurs outside the female's body.

- Easy does it! The male sweeps the fertilized eggs onto the female's back with his feet.

- The eggs sink into hollows in the skin of the female's back. There they will be safe, moist, and warm.

- What a mom! The eggs stay on the female's back for three to five months until they develop into tiny frogs.

The young frogs hatch from eggs carried on their mother's back.

? What animals, other than mammals, take care of their young for an extended period of time? How do they do this?

The Expert Says...

"The Surinam toad's aquatic lifestyle means that it can rarely leave the water. Although this provides needed protection from predators, hidden threats lie in the water. There are many pollutants in the water. My research shows that these chemicals stress these animals and hurt their development. It's not easy being green!"

— Christina Fridgen, researcher, Biology Department, Trent University

Take Note

We ranked the Surinam toad #4 on our list because it takes care of its young longer than most other frogs. We also liked this frog's other un-frog-like ways. Its great camouflage is an added bonus!

- Different animals have different ways of looking after their eggs. Which way do you think is best? Why?

5   4   3   2   1

3 MUDSKIPPERS

Indian mudskipper —
a fish out of water!

DESCRIPTION: A type of bony fish from the goby family that is found only in tropical and subtropical regions

COOL TOOL: A mudskipper can survive on land thanks to skin that can take in air and elbow-like front fins that help it to scoot along the ground.

Meet the mudskipper — a fish with "elbows" that can hop around on land. Yep, really! True to their name, mudskippers spend a lot of their time hopping around on the mud flats left behind by tides. These unique fish are amphibious, which means they can breathe both in water and on land thanks to some unusual adaptations.

A mudskipper's bag of tricks also includes some interesting behavior. It makes mud pellets in its mouth and uses them to build burrows with tall towers. The mudskipper also has some fancy courting rituals. In some species of mudskippers, the male will stick out its colorful back fin and dance and wriggle around to attract a female. It will also pop in and out of its burrow as if to say, "Come on in!"

 Why do you think a mudskipper makes towers on top of its burrow? Hint: it may be for the same reason that towers were built in castles in olden days.

MUDSKIPPERS

Quick Fact

To protect its territory, a male will open its mouth wide. Its color darkens and its back fin straightens up. Sometimes the males will chase one another or even fight by locking mouths — a very strange wrestling match indeed!

LOOKING GOOD!

Mudskippers are mud-colored and range in size from two to 12 inches. Their front fins bend forward in an arm-like fashion, making mudskippers look as if they have elbows! They also have frog-like eyes that can be drawn back into their heads.

? Mudskippers have eyes on the top of their heads. This is more frog-like than fish-like. Why do you think they evolved this way?

? Mudskipper males defend their territories very aggressively. Why do you think they do that?

WHERE IN THE WORLD?

Mudskippers are not big on cold weather. They live in the tropical and subtropical areas around the Indian Ocean. These muck-loving fish are usually found in mangrove swamps or other muddy areas left behind by the tides.

mangrove: *trees that grow along riverbanks and ocean coastlines in tropical areas*

FINE DINING

Some mudskippers are carnivorous, meaning they eat mostly meat. This includes insects, worms, and small shellfish like shrimp and crab. Other mudskippers go "veggie" and eat algae.

SURVIVAL KIT

In addition to their cool talent of being able to breathe on both land and air, mudskippers are darn good skippers. They move themselves forward on land by pushing with both fins at once. They can also make impressive jumps of more than 40 inches by using their tails like springs!

Quick Fact

Some kinds of mudskippers can actually climb roots and plants! These squirrelly mudskippers have back fins acting like suction cups that prevent them from falling.

The Expert Says...

"Mudskippers are masters of visual communication. The species living on the mud flats exhibit huge fins that they expand and hold like the flags of an embassy. Those living inside the dark forests instead have smaller fins with patches of color. They rapidly raise and lower their fins like the small flags used by the deck crew of aircraft carriers!

— Gianluca Polgar, researcher, Biology Department, University of Rome

embassy: *ambassador's office in a foreign country*

10   **9**   **8**   **7**   **6**

Mudskippers carry air around with them in much the same way we carry air around in scuba tanks. This fact chart explains how they use air to survive.

HERE'S HOW:

1. When a mudskipper moves on land, it holds a bubble of air in its mouth. This seals its gills, which it uses for breathing in the water. The air in its mouth is then slowly absorbed into its body through the linings of its mouth.

Quick Fact

Mudskippers have a unique way of stopping their eyes from drying out on land. They carry small pools of water at the bottom of their eye sockets!

2. A mudskipper has another trick to help it survive on land. It can also absorb oxygen through its skin! But it must keep its skin moist to do this. No wonder it is always rolling around in puddles!

3. A mudskipper also needs to breathe in its burrow, when it's covered by the tide. To do this, a mudskipper gulps up air and carries it into its burrow to create an underground air pocket to last out the tide!

Take Note

This fish can survive on both land and water with ease. With that in mind, and some of the mudskipper's quirky mating and house-building behavior, we couldn't help but rank this little animal high on our list at #3.
• Do you think these traits are enough to rank the mudskipper higher than the Surinam toad? Why?

5   4   **3**   2   1

See for yourself why this bat is also known as "the flying fox."

PALLID BAT–© J. & P. BERQUIST/ANIMALS ANIMALS

DESCRIPTION: A mammal from the Chiroptera order that includes two subgroups: megabats and microbats

COOL TOOL: Bats are the only flying mammal — they have wings! Their sense of echolocation is nothing to sneeze at either.

Bats are the only mammals that have wings and can fly. Not impressed? Well, imagine seeing your neighbor's cat flying past your window! A flying mammal is pretty special.

Bats' shrew-like ancestors once lived in the trees. These guys would jump from branch to branch catching bugs. The ones that had flaps of skin between their limbs could glide a bit and were better bug catchers. Eating better meant they probably lived longer and had more young — many of which inherited their parents' floppy skin. Over thousands of years, those flaps of skin got larger and larger until they developed into the wings that we see on bats today.

A bat's built-in sonar is a pretty handy adaptation too. Some bats' sonar is so accurate that it can detect an itsy-bitsy fruit fly almost 100 feet away. Not bad!

shrew: *small, mouse-like mammal with a long snout, related to moles*
sonar: *ability to use sound waves to figure out how far away something is*

 In New Zealand, there is more food on the ground for bats than there is in the air. Why do you think bats there are more similar to their shrew-like ancestors than bats elsewhere?

BATS

LOOKING GOOD!

Bats have small, furry bodies with long, stick-like legs. The fingers on their forelimbs are very long and their thin wings spread from finger to finger and down to their legs. They have a thumb on each forearm that's not attached to their wings. The thumb has a large claw used to help them climb. Bats' sizes vary by species.

> **?** Bats have very thin, bony limbs. Why do you think they need to have such small legs? How do they get away with having almost no muscles on their limbs?

WHERE IN THE WORLD?

Bats live almost everywhere in the world except the far North and South (which are too cold). "Home" to a bat might be a cave, mine, tunnel, crevice, or tree. Wherever they are, you can usually find them hanging out in huge bat communities since they are very social.

FINE DINING

Most kinds of bats eat insects, but there are a few vegetarian species that just eat plants. Of course, there are also those notorious blood-feeding vampire bats!

Quick Fact

The Mexican free-tailed bat wins the award for being the friendliest bat. This bat lives in huge bat communities. In fact, one cave can contain up to 40 million bats. That's a larger population than California!

SURVIVAL KIT

Bats are amazing fliers thanks to their unique wings. A bat's wings are more flexible than a bird's. By bending its wings into different shapes, a bat can quickly change its flying direction and weave and dive through the air after its prey. A bat's built-in sonar equipment also makes it a better hunter.

The Expert Says...

" Bats are the second largest group of mammals, but out of 1,100 species only three are vampires. These live in Mexico and Central and South America. "

— Dr. Bill Schutt, Ph.D., Long Island University and the American Museum of Natural History

FLYING BAT–©JOE MCDONALD/ANIMALS ANIMALS; VAMPIRE BAT–© ZIG LESZCZYNSKI/ANIMALS ANIMALS; BACKGROUND–SHUTTERSTOCK

10   **9**   **8**   **7**   **6**

GETTING AROUND USING SOUND

"Echolocation" means using "echoes" to "locate" things. This ability is important for bats since they do most of their hunting in the dark. (There are fewer competing hunters and more insects out at night.) This diagram shows how bats get around using sound:

Bats let out squeaks and clicks through their mouths or nostrils. These sounds are so high that humans can't hear them.

As in the picture above, the sound waves spread away from the bat. The sound waves are like ripples in a pond: they become larger as they move away.

The sound waves hit objects (hopefully a nice juicy bug) and are bounced back to the bat.

When the bat gets the sound wave back, it gets a lot of information from it (like the size, shape, and distance of the object). That helps the bat's brain to form a picture of the object in almost the same way as when it sees something.

As the bat gets closer to its prey, it makes its squeaks higher and higher. This increases the number of sound waves per second (from about 5 to 200). This helps the bat to get more precise information about the bug's location and zoom in on it.

Quick Fact

Talk about sticking your foot in your mouth! A bat actually scoops up flying insects with the membrane between its hind legs and then passes them forward to its mouth.

Take Note

Bats adapted from one environment to another (from tree-living to being airborne). They are the only flying mammal and have unique wings. We also thought the bat's sense of echolocation was pretty cool. These things, and our favoritism for fellow mammals, all helped us to put the bat at #2 on our list.
- Several other animals on our list, including the mudskipper at #3, also adapted from one environment to another. Do you think the bat's sense of echolocation is enough to give it the edge over the other animals on our list? Why or why not?

5   4   3   2   1

1 PLATYPUS

A duck's bill on a mammal — now that's a strange adaptation!

PLATYPUS–NATIONAL GEOGRAPHIC/GETTY IMAGES

ES

DESCRIPTION: Semi-aquatic mammal found in eastern Australia and Tasmania

COOL TOOL: It isn't easy picking the coolest part of a platypus! Trust us, we tried. How about its electric signal-seeking snout? Or the male platypus's poisonous ankle spurs?

The platypus is so zany it just had to top our list. In fact, the first time scientists saw one, they figured it was a hoax. They thought someone had glued a duck's feet and bill to a small mammal! With its bizarre looks, the platypus is one special animal.

The platypus is unusual because it is the only mammal that lays eggs. A female platypus carries her eggs around inside her for about 28 days. Once the eggs are laid, it takes about 10 days for them to hatch.

And wait till you hear how a platypus finds its food! (Hint: it's similar to how sharks do it.) You haven't lived until you've learned about the platypus and its amazing adaptations. Read on and learn all about this incredible animal.

 When scientists first discovered the platypus, it was so unusual they thought it might be a hoax. Why do you think scientists might have thought this?

PLATYPUSES

LOOKING GOOD!

What can we say? Add a duck-like bill and four webbed feet to a beaver and you've pretty much got a platypus. But a platypus is smaller than a beaver. The average length of a platypus is between 16 and 24 inches.

WHERE IN THE WORLD?

The amazing platypus lives in Tasmania and eastern Australia. Fossils of animals related to the platypus have been found. But today, the platypus has no living relatives. It truly is one-of-a-kind.

FINE DINING

Shrimps, insects, crayfish, and worms are some of the favorite food of a platypus.

SURVIVAL KIT

The platypus comes with great built-in swimming gear. It's a good thing, too. In order for a platypus to get enough to eat, it needs to be in the water looking for food about 12 hours a day. A platypus uses its front limbs like canoe paddles to move through the water. Its back feet help with steering. Other nifty platypus equipment includes thick brown fur that keeps a warm layer of air next to its skin and a flat tail that stores extra fat.

The platypus is nocturnal, so it does most of its swimming at night. What other ways do you think it avoids getting into trouble with hungry predators?

Quick Fact

It may be cute and furry but a platypus is not all fun and games — at least not the male ones! A male platypus has spurs on its ankles that can eject poison. This poison is strong enough to kill a small animal and would cause an adult human great pain.

Only a male platypus has venomous spurs. These spurs produce more venom during the breeding season. Why do you think that is?

The Expert Says...

"The platypus is a difficult species for a scientist to study. It is mainly active at night and spends a lot of time either underwater or underground in burrows. It is a small, solitary animal that blends in with its surroundings and leaves few tracks. ... It's hard work, but very exciting to discover more about the world's strangest mammal."

— Dr. Melody Serena, conservation biologist, Australian Platypus Conservancy

10   9   8   7   6

A SHOCKINGLY SUPERIOR SNOUT

With all its wacky adaptations, it should come as no surprise that a platypus can "see" with its snout. That comes in handy since a platypus keeps both its eyes and ears closed when it swims. So just how does it use its bill to find its prey? By electrolocation of course! That's the same sense that sharks sometimes use to locate food. This list shows how it works in a platypus:

- When an animal moves, its muscles give out electric signals. Our muscles give out these signals too. Humans don't have the ability to "see" or "feel" these signals, but the platypus can!

- The skin of the platypus's snout is covered with tiny receivers that can pick up these electronic signals. When a platypus is looking for food, it swims quickly across the river, moving its bill-like snout from side to side.

- When a worm or fish moves, the platypus's bill tunes in on the signals being released by their muscles. Even if an animal is buried, the platypus can still pick up the signals.

Quick Fact

Dig this: a platypus's webbed feet are also good for burrowing. In fact, a mother platypus can dig a tunnel up to 65 feet long to raise her young in. That's longer than a school bus!

- By comparing how strong the signal is on different parts of its snout, a platypus can figure out where the signal is coming from. Then it can snatch up its prey.

- If a platypus doesn't come across any signals, it may try digging up the riverbed with its snout to get its prey moving. When the prey tries to escape, it seals its own fate. Even with its eyes closed, the platypus "sees" the signals from its moving prey and gobbles it up. Dinner is served!

Take Note

The platypus is on the top of our list of amazing adaptations. Not only does it have a lot of incredible equipment — from its webbed feet and flat tail to the male's poisonous spurs — but it is also one of the only living mammals that lays eggs. Plus, its sense of electrolocation is shocking. Looking like it was put together by a mad scientist helped its ranking, too.
- What do you think? Does the platypus deserve to be ranked #1? If not, what would your #1 choice be? Explain your answer.

5   4   3   2   1

We Thought ...

Here are the criteria we used in ranking the 10 most amazing adaptations in nature.

The adaptation:
- Was surprising
- Was effective in helping the animal or plant survive
- Evolved over time to help the animal or plant live
- Had an interesting or unusual appearance
- Helped the animal or plant survive in more than one type of environment
- Included a unique mating habit

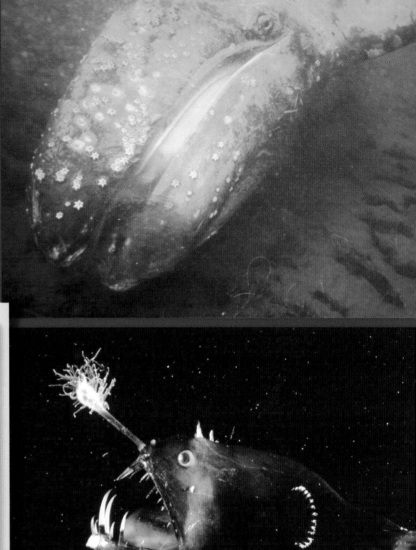

What Do You Think?

1. Do you agree with our ranking? If you don't, try ranking them yourself. Justify your ranking with data from your own research and reasoning. You may refer to our criteria, or you may want to draw up your own list of criteria.

2. Here are three other animals with amazing adaptations that we considered but in the end did not include in our top 10 list: the naked mole rat, the camel, and the flying squirrel.
   • Find out more about them. Do you think they should have made our list? Give reasons for your response.
   • Are there other animals that you think should have made our list? Explain your choices.

Index